FLYING CAN BE FUN

FLYING CAN BE FUN

Illustrated by DICK LOCHER
Text by MICHAEL KILIAN

PELICAN PUBLISHING COMPANY

GRETNA 1985

Library of Congress Cataloging in Publication Data

Kilian, Michael.
  Flying can be fun.

  1. Aeronautics—Anecdotes, facetiae, satire,
etc. I. Locher, Dick. II. Title.
PN6231.A4K54   1985   818'.5402   85-5677
ISBN 0-88289-449-8 (pbk.)

Manufactured in the United States of America
Published by Pelican Publishing Company, Inc.
1101 Monroe Street, Gretna, Louisiana 70053

For Laura C. Kilian, who as a barnstorming-era wing-walker called "the Nerve Gal" used to hang from biplanes by a silk stocking,

And for Joe Locher, who failed in his ardent wish to get into World War I combat when his British SE-5 stalled out at 1,000 feet and crashed on a training flight.

We are eternally grateful they both survived.

Am I here?

Charles A. Lindbergh, upon arriving in Paris after his solo flight across the Atlantic. (Also the favorite phrase of student pilots upon completing their first cross-country flights.)

FLYING CAN BE FUN

Airplane . . . An invention of two bicycle mechanics from Ohio perfected on the sands of the Outer Banks at Kitty Hawk, North Carolina. Precursor of the Frisbee.

Abeam . . . A fix, point, or object approximately ninety degrees to the right or left of an aircraft's flight path, most often a runway.

Abort . . . Most commonly used command by flight instructors to student pilots, often retroactively made to mothers of student pilots.

Aerial . . . That part of the aircraft most frequently broken off during walk-around pre-flight inspection to see if anything is broken off.

Aero . . . That part of the atmosphere which lies over Great Britain.

Aerodrome . . . English word for airport. What you'd expect from a country that gives its airplanes names like Gypsy Moth and Fairey Battle Bomber.

Aileron . . . A hinged control surface on the wing which scares the hell out of airline passengers when it moves. Also, an eron that is sick.

Airfoil . . . That part of the airplane which foils the pilot's efforts to fly it—usually anything connected to the stick.

Airplane . . . An invention of two bicycle mechanics from Ohio perfected on the sands of the Outer Banks at Kitty Hawk, North Carolina. Precursor of the Frisbee.

Air traffic controller . . . A federal employee, usually a retired tobacco auctioneer, assigned to a major airport to keep aircraft from landing in unison by giving rapid instructions over the radio, most of which mean to go away and come back again—preferably after the air traffic controller is off duty.

Aileron

Airworthy . . . The line on the clipboard checksheet that the ground mechanic marks after finishing a pint of whiskey.

Aisle . . . The narrowest part of any jetliner, usually equal to the widest part of a flight attendant.

Alternate airport . . . Designation given to New York's LaGuardia Airport for a flight bound for Chicago's O'Hare Airport from New York's Kennedy Airport when the flight is over Fort Wayne, Indiana.

Altitude . . . That part of the atmosphere above a pilot whose engine has just conked out.

Aisle

Attitude . . . The pilot's mental outlook. A pilot who shouts and screams if his engine conks out is said to have a bad attitude, not to speak of altitude.

Automatic pilot . . . What advertising executives and other trendies think they are just by wearing brown leather World War II bomber-crew jackets they bought after seeing the movie *The Right Stuff*.

Balloon . . . Antiquated eighteenth-century invention still flown by fanatical aerial-sports enthusiasts ignorant of fact that Newton's theory of gravity has already been proved.

Automatic Pilot

Bank . . . That which keeps most aircraft flying, depending upon the interest rates.

Biplane . . . The lane on airport access roads used by bips.

Blast fence . . . Popular substitute for aluminum siding on houses in neighborhoods adjoining airports.

Boundary lights . . . Airport lights visible from distances as great as five and sometimes even six feet.

Biplane

Bravo . . . Phonetic alphabet for letter *B*. Seldom transmitted to student pilots on first landing.

Broken . . . Weather forecast term for cloud cover with large openings. Also, what happens to aircraft when forecast is wrong.

Buffeting . . . Atmospheric disturbance that occurs when flight attendants are serving dinner. Origin of the phrase *buffet dinner,* usually meaning, "eat where you can, even if on floor—or ceiling."

Buffeting

Bulkhead . . . Term used by pilots to describe that part of cockpit area beneath the copilot's hat.

Bunt . . . An aerobatic maneuver in which a plane dives from level flight to an inverted position, completing the first half of an outside loop. A favorite of student pilots responding to the command, "Get the nose down!"

Canopy . . . The useful transparent covering of a power plane or glider that protects the pilot from the wind while the sun is heating the cockpit to approximately 900 degrees.

Canopy

CAVU (Ceiling And Visibility Unlimited) . . . Atmospheric condition occurring almost as frequently as an eclipse of the sun and noted for the spectacular view it affords pilots. Also, sound made by birds flying in formation just before a pilot absorbed by a spectacular view runs into them.

Ceiling . . . The height of the cloud base above the ground, usually one-half the height of the nearest radio transmitter (see IFR). Also, the surface toward which a wife travels when informed her husband is going to take up flying.

Celestial navigation . . . Flight procedure used by pilots who have lost their instruments; usually performed on knees.

Celestial Navigation

Center of gravity . . . The exact midpoint of the suitcase that is sliding around back there in the luggage compartment.

Check list . . . A list of those items a pilot has to write checks for to get fixed before taking off.

Chop . . . Airline pilot parlance for turbulence, especially on Asian flights. Also, what the pilots are probably getting to eat instead of the plastic glop being served to passengers.

Circle . . . Approach pattern used by aircraft within 12,000 miles of Chicago at 5:00 P.M. on Fridays.

Clearance . . . Strange, indecipherable mumbling sound occasionally heard over earphones of pilots prior to collision with other taxiing aircraft.

Chop

Cockpit . . . A confined place where two chickens fight each other, especially when they can't find the airport in a rainstorm.

Cocktail . . . Refreshment consisting of ice-filled plastic glass and small laboratory bottle containing alcohol and topped with adult-proof metal cap. Almost always brought to passenger approximately six minutes before touchdown.

Compass . . . An amusing device in the instrument panel that comically spins back and forth when you're trying to find an airport in a rainstorm.

Compass

Concorde . . . A B-1 bomber designed to carry rich people, usually across the Atlantic Ocean at stratospheric altitudes and even higher ticket prices. Also, an Anglo-French phrase meaning any agreement between France and Britain that will guarantee a loss of billions of dollars.

Contact . . . Expression used by the ground crew when struck in the hand by propellor they've been turning manually to start engine.

Controlled airspace . . . Synonym for entire United States of America.

Coordinates . . . Flying clothes worn by fashionable female pilots. Also, points on a map or chart usually indicating a Coca-Cola ring or grease stain.

Contact

Course . . . Popular alternate landing field marked by fairways and greens. Curiously, pilots who land on them are said to be "off course."

Crab . . . A landing technique used to compensate for crosswinds. Usually fails, making pilot crabby.

Cross below altitude . . . Instruction given by air traffic controller, usually taken by student pilots to mean "get the aircraft underground as soon as possible."

Crosswind . . . A wind that is angry with you.

Defense Visual Flight Rules . . . Federal aviation rules that allow military pilots to shoot down stray general aviation aircraft as soon as they are sighted.

Course

Departure time . . . Archaic phrase dating back to passenger-railroad days indicating a moment in time approximately three hours before takeoff.

Dinner . . . Strange plastic substance served to passengers on evening flights. Likely to be the reheated strange substance rejected by passengers on midday flights.

Direction finder . . . Anyone who answers a student pilot's radio transmission.

Dinner

Dive . . . Landing maneuver favored by student pilots running out of runway. (This is exceeded in popularity only by *Strangle,* a landing maneuver favored by flight instructors when student pilot fails to respond to a friendly, helpful suggestion, such as, "Get the nose down!")

Dividend . . . Archaic expression, at one time applicable to owners of airline stock.

Downwind leg . . . The one to be especially careful of when landing after long flights at small airports without restroom facilities.

Dive

Drag . . . Force which opposes forward motion of aircraft when pilot forgets to untie tiedown.

Drag chute . . . Emergency escape slide near pilot's window. Automatically opens up when copilot shows up in women's clothes.

E . . . Letter pointed to by many a compass needle when aircraft is actually heading *S*.

Elevation . . . Height of ground above sea level. When flying in the Rockies, usually something 3,000 feet above you.

Drag

Elevator . . . Description of flight characteristics of aircraft in thunderstorms.

ELT (Emergency Locator Transmitter) . . . Self-contained radio transmitter automatically activated by crash. Emits a distinctive variable tone on emergency frequencies 121.5 and 243.0 megahertz, unless pilot has let the battery run down. Also, strange word that appears on malfunctioning overhead Fasten Seat Belt sign.

Empennage . . . What happens when you drop your ballpoint pen in the carburetor.

Elevator

En route flight advisory . . . Air traffic control service provided to pilots to inform them of why they shouldn't have taken off.

Error . . . Basic component of every flight since Wright Brothers wrecked their aircraft at Kitty Hawk in 1903 in an attempt to repeat their historic first flight.

Execute . . . To carry out a command or procedure, as in, "I'll kill that sonofabitch who turned in front of me on final!"

Executive class . . . Section of jetliner set aside for small, noisy children; women with large packages; unwashed youths; suspicious-looking bearded men who speak in foreign languages and eat food out of their pockets; diseased persons with hacking coughs; and others let on at the last minute.

Error

43

Exit . . . Door at opposite end of an airliner.

Fairing . . . Any part of an aircraft used to streamline its outline and reduce drag, such as the bowler hats worn by Wright Brothers at Kitty Hawk. Also, what a pilot might call a copilot who showed up in women's clothes.

FARs (Federal Aviation Regulations) . . . Closely related to Farsi, language of Iran.

Feathered propellor . . . A propellor whose blades have been rotated so that the leading and trailing edges are nearly parallel after collision with a flock of birds.

Feathered Propellor

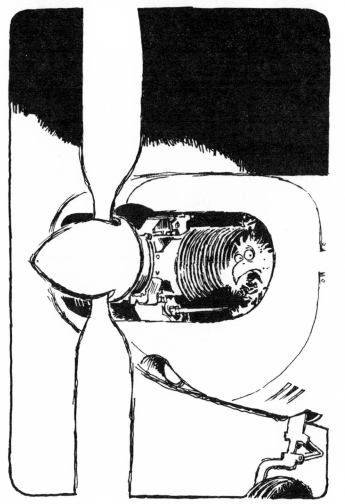

Feeder route . . . Short flight from an outlying city; notable for its lack of meal service.

Final approach . . . Many a seasoned pilot's last landing. Also, many a student pilot's first landing.

Fix . . . A position determined by visual reference or navigational aid and communicated to air traffic controller with prefix "I'm in a . . ."

Fixed wing . . . Nomenclature for part of aircraft flown by student pilots that is finally ready for next student pilot.

Flap . . . What some airline passengers start when they see what looks like part of the wing sliding off on landing approach.

Fixed Wing

Flight service station . . . Official designation given to airports that are closed.

Formation . . . Type of precision flying used by two aircraft when they discover they have turned on final approach for the runway at the same time.

Fuel venting . . . Term to explain to passengers why strange fluid is inadvertently streaming off of wing surface. Also, why many rural communities have become No Smoking sections.

G . . . Measurement of the pull of gravity. A pilot who is in an extremely tight diving turn, for example, will exclaim, *"Geeeeeeeeeeee!"*

G

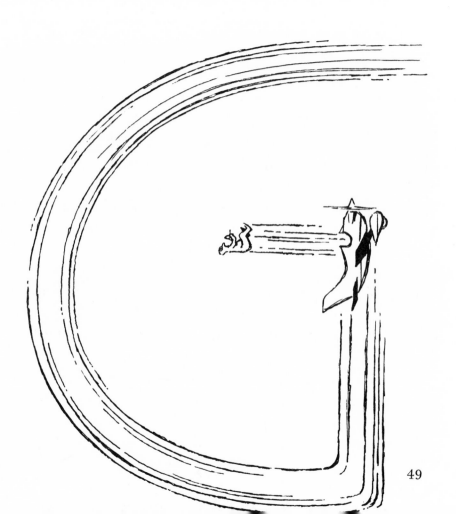

Gate . . . What airliners wait an hour or more for after arriving twenty minutes early. Also, the door on the opposite end of the departure area from where you're sitting.

General aviation . . . What Lieutenant Aviation would have become if he hadn't taxied his thirty-five-million-dollar F-15 into a C-5A transport.

Glide . . . Sustained forward flight in which speed is maintained only by the loss of altitude. A jetliner that has lost power still has the ability to glide to the nearest airport, only to find a Cessna 150 is using the runway.

Glider . . . Aircraft flown by pilots who know you only go around once in life.

General Aviation

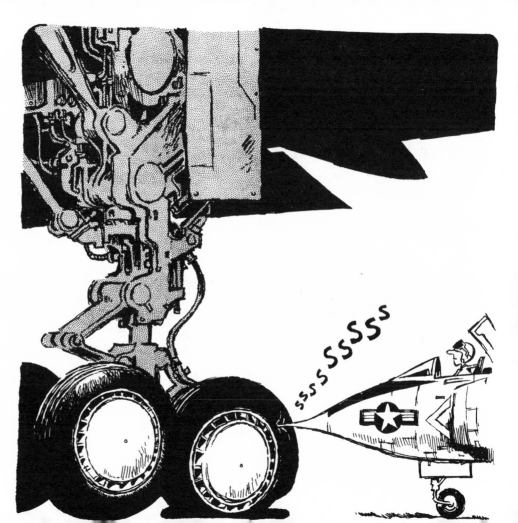

Glide slope . . . Where not to park aircraft without tiedowns.

Go around . . . Maneuver often suggested by flight instructor when student pilot has landing approach set up perfectly if it weren't for the Piper 140 turning final just twenty feet ahead.

Ground clutter . . . Small blips appearing on radar screen indicating empty bottles, beer cans, and broken pieces of boundary lights.

Ground loop . . . Popular landing maneuver used for crosswinds.

Ground speed . . . What a pilot on landing discovers airspeed becomes.

Ground Clutter

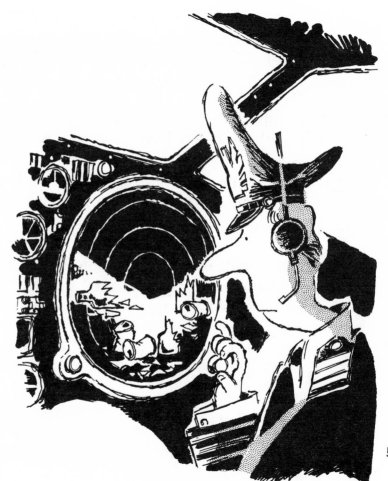

HAA (Height Above Airport) . . . As in, "You were supposed to touch down back there, HAA, HAA, HAA!"

Helicopter . . . Wingless hovering aircraft used by radio stations to inform motorists caught in traffic jams that they are caught in traffic jams.

Helipad . . . Hangar used by hippie helicopters. Also, that portion of ground or building roof used by helicopters for landing and taking off.

Heliport . . . That portion of presumed helipad that helicopter pilot discovers is actually water.

Helicopter

Hertz . . . A measure of frequency, except during the Friday night rush when the lines at the car-rental counter are long.

Holding fix . . . Radio communication frequently heard among pilots in southern Florida.

Homing . . . Approach procedure used by pilots who abandon instruments and follow what looks like a carrier pigeon.

Horsepower . . . Measurement of power sometimes required to extricate small aircraft from farmers' muddy fields.

Hot . . . A pilot able to perform dangerous maneuvers with dash and daring. Also, an extremely fast landing. Also, an air traffic controller witnessing it all.

Hot

Hotel . . . The letter *H* as pronounced in phonetic alphabet. Most often heard in intercom conversations between pilots and flight attendants.

IAS (Indicated Air Speed) . . . Usually, what is shown on a malfunctioning air speed indicator.

Icing . . . What frequently happens to pilots who think that flying through winter thunderstorms is a piece of cake.

Ident . . . Warning issued by landing pilots to those taxiing on active runways.

IFR (Idiot Flight Rules) . . . Exclamation frequently uttered by pilots flying on instruments in heavy cloud (see VFR).

IFR
(Idiot Flight Rules)

ILS (Idiot Landing System) . . . The ultimate result of following idiot flight rules.

Immelmann turn . . . Complicated World War I aerial combat maneuver invented by German ace Max Immelmann shortly before he was killed. It involves climb, turn, and inverted flight that puts aircraft on tail of aircraft that had been following. Popular landing approach of student pilots making first landing.

Induced drag . . . When a copilot is made to put on women's clothes against his will.

Initial approach . . . That point in a landing when a student pilot is usually told to go around.

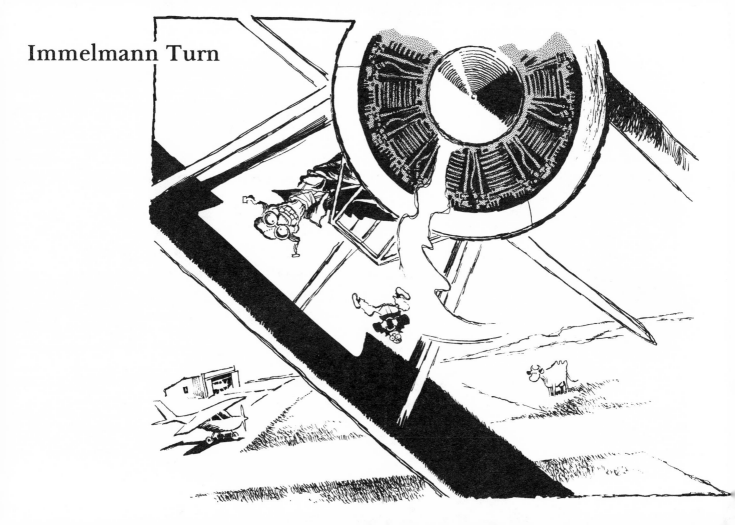

Immelmann Turn

Inner marker...What most frequently shows up on instrument landings when a pilot is looking for the outer marker.

I say again . . . Radio transmission used most frequently by pilots who are also politicians.

Jenny . . . Rickety biplane used by daredevil barnstormers to dampen public support for aviation for at least a decade after World War I.

Jet . . . Device on modern passenger airliners used for removing large migratory birds from airways.

Jet-assisted takeoff . . . Rapid takeoff procedure used by a general-aviation pilot who finds himself on a runway in front of a Boeing 737.

Jenny

Jet set . . . Name of a rich people's tennis match begun at Wimbledon and concluded at Forest Hills with help of the Concorde.

Jetstream . . . Any airspace within 1,000 miles of Washington National Airport at 5:00 P.M. on Fridays.

Joint-use restricted area . . . Smoking section of airliner used by long-haired passengers.

Joy stick . . . Smoking material used in airliner joint-use restricted areas.

Jump . . . Pilot maneuver used to get out of a flat spin.

Jet Set

Kablooommm!!!! . . . What thunder fifty miles away sounds like to student pilot.

Keep 'em flying . . . 1941 flying epic starring Abbott and Costello, the immortal Carol Bruce, and the even more immortal Martha Raye. The latter two played twins, quite possibly Lycoming radials. Frequently shown on no-frills transatlantic charter flights.

Kilohertz . . . Radio frequency. Also, rental car popular in southern Florida.

Kinesthesia . . . The sense that detects and estimates motion without reference to vision or hearing. Often used by student pilots.

King air . . . Commodious executive propjet favored by state governors and other VIPs who think that riding in such an expensive aircraft makes them that.

King Air

Kit . . . Permanently unassembled small aircraft.

Kite . . . Maneuver performed when writing checks to pay for airplane.

Kiwi . . . Wingless and thus much happier bird.

Knot . . . A measurement of speed. For example, an airliner landing at a speed of 250 miles per hour will tie passengers' stomachs into at least seventeen knots.

Kool-aid . . . On feeder airlines, usually the only beverage mixer available when you ask the flight attendant for a Bloody Mary.

Knot

Lateral separation . . . Explanation for a funny blast of cold air coming into the cockpit near wing joint.

Lavatory . . . Small cubicles on jetliners available only during landing approach and violent thunderstorms.

Leading edge . . . That part of the aircraft that hits other aircraft while taxiing. (*See* Trailing Edge.)

Lift . . . A phenomenon of nature that turns a parked aircraft upside down if it is not tied down properly during windstorms.

Leading Edge

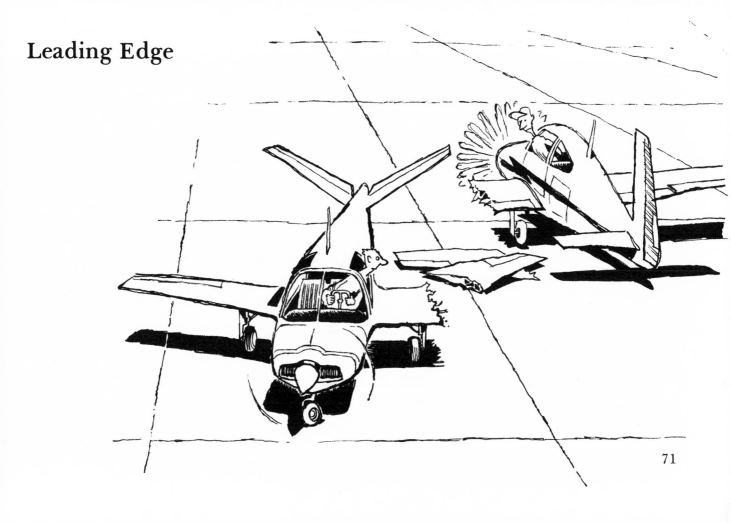

Localizer . . . Any type of major storm that convinces you to cancel your flight.

Log . . . A small rectangular notebook used to record lies.

Longeron . . . A longitudinal structural member of the fuselage used when a shorteron won't reach far enough.

Magnetic heading . . . That which makes your compass needle swing amusingly back and forth. Also, a direction approximately 90 degrees from where your nose is pointed.

Longeron

Magneto . . . Spanish term meaning "your mag is very clean and neat."

Minimum fuel . . . What pilots for shoestring commuter airlines often buy when pulling up to avgas pumps.

Minimums . . . Air traffic controller euphemism for dense, impenetrable fog.

Missed Approach . . . A favorite maneuver among glider pilots, used when a landing approach cannot be completed, necessitating a climb to altitude for a go-around.

Missed Approach

Mitchell . . . World War II twin-engined light bomber named for Colonel William "Billy" Mitchell, an early advocate of air power who claimed the airplane would come to dominate warfare, only to be proved wrong by the invention of the B-1 bomber, the C-5 transport, the F/A-18 fighter-bomber, and other lemons.

MLS (Microwave Landing System) . . . Used by pilots who are back in the galley chatting with flight attendants when aircraft is about to land.

Mode . . . Term used by pilots in the Lafayette Escadrille for what they had to land in during rainy weather.

Mode

Monocoque . . . A coquepit that only fits one.

Monoplane . . . A biplane at the conclusion of a bunt.

MSL . . . Mean sea level, or what sea level can be if you fail to set your altimeter properly.

NA . . . Not authorized. Also, *Nah, Nix, Nope, Nein, No-No,* and @%$#!*&+&**#@!

Nacelle . . . French term for malfunctioning battery.

National Airport...Inordinately congested airport in Washington, D.C., whose Potomac River approach was used by Korean War pilots practicing to bomb bridges at Toko-ri.

Navaids...Bandaids used to hold navigational dials in place on instrument panel in some old aircraft.

Navigable Airspace...All airspace above 100,000 feet at 5:00 P.M. on Fridays.

Negative Contact...Used by pilots to inform air traffic controller they cannot contact air traffic controller. Also, the result of physical contact with other aircraft.

National Airport

Night . . . The time between the end of evening civil twilight and the beginning of morning civil twilight. Also known as dusk to dawn, hours of darkness, and the period when a student pilot on his first cross-country flight begins to wonder if he might have overflown his destination.

Nosewheel . . . That part of a Piper Cub that a student pilot discovers too late is on the other end.

Notams . . . FAA Notices to Airmen.

Numerous Targets Vicinity . . . A traffic advisory issued to advise pilots that targets on the radar scope are too numerous to issue individually. (See Pearl Harbor, early use of radar.)

Nosewheel

Obstruction . . . Any high-rise building that refuses to get out of the way.

Occupied . . . Aeronautical term for lavatory.

Oleo . . . A shock-absorbing strut in which the spring action bends like warm margarine.

Omni . . . Radio gizmo that jiggles when you're directly over a city even though you still can't see the airport.

Omni

Option Approach . . . An approach requested and conducted by a pilot that will result in either touch-and-go, missed approach, low approach, stop-and-go, full stop landing, ground loop, touch-and-Dutch-roll, stop-and-Immelmann-turn, touch-and-bounce, three-bank-side-pocket-shot, inverted taxi, or some other fascinating tale to tell around the hangar after it's rebuilt.

Orientation . . . What happened to Northwest Airlines when it became Northwest Orient.

Oshkosh . . . A town in Wisconsin that is the site of the annual Experimental Aircraft Association Fly-In. It is believed to have been named after the sound that most experimental aircraft engines make.

Oshkosh

Over . . . Radio transmission made by pilot describing flight in minimums.

Overhead Approach . . . An elliptical landing pattern used by Navy carrier pilots who are nervous about flying near pitching deck. Also, a favorite of commercial airline pilots who make landings at South America's many airports built inside volcanoes.

Overshoot . . . Hobby of many farmers with shotguns who live near general-aviation airports.

Over-the-top . . . Above the layer of clouds. In the Midwest during the thunderstorm season, this means a landing on the moon.

Overhead Approach

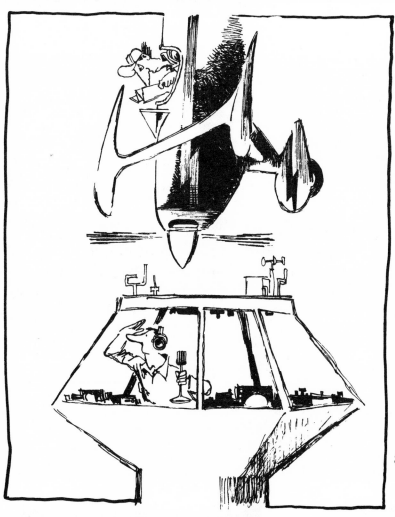

Pattern . . . Official government terminology describing aircraft aimlessly milling about near landing fields.

Phonetic alphabet . . . A linguistic system believed to have been invented by the ancient Phoenicians. Makes alphabet letters even more incomprehensible over the radio by transforming them into peculiar words: Alpha for *A,* Charlie for *C,* Foxtrot for *F,* Victor for *V,* Zulu for *Z,* etc. Use of phonetic-alphabet word for *K*—"Kilo"— has gotten some pilots in trouble with the Drug Enforcement Agency in southern Florida.

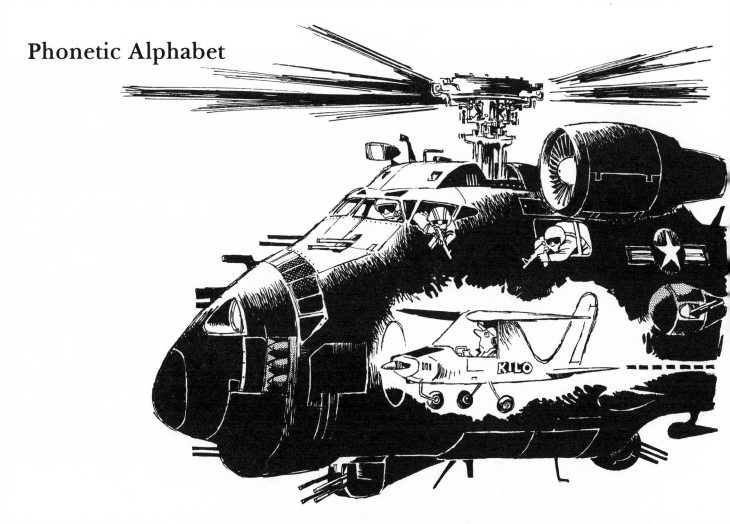

Phonetic Alphabet

Pitch . . . One of the three movements of an aircraft on its axis, often manifested by presence of flight attendant on ceiling of tail section when pilot accidentally jars control wheel with elbow.

Pitot tube . . . *Not,* on long flights, something into which to pitot.

Precision approach . . . A mythical aerial maneuver (See overhead approach).

Pre-flight . . . A procedure involving detailed inspection of aircraft and its condition. Usually takes longer than the actual flight—especially if a major part of it is skipped.

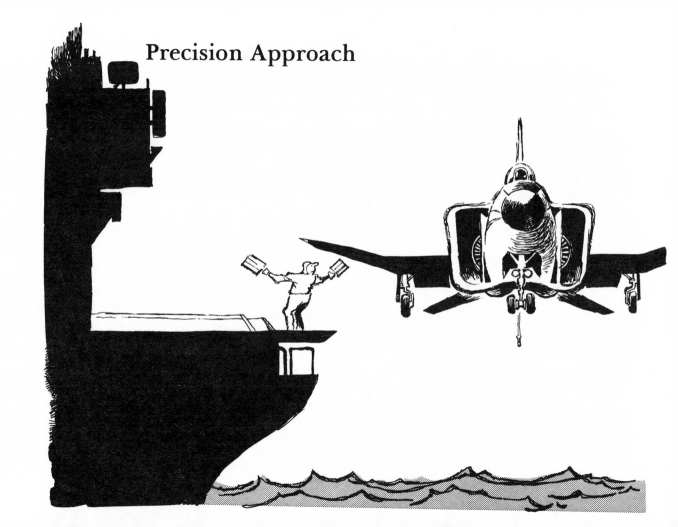

Precision Approach

President's Plane Is Missing . . . 1971 flying epic about Andrews Air Force Base air traffic controller who needs new glasses.

Pylon . . . A pile of crashed aircraft at one end of an air-race course.

Q.N.H. . . . International code for air pressure at sea level. Used by pilots trying to reset altimeters. Can also mean "where are the life rafts?"

Q-Planes . . . 1939 Laurence Olivier flying epic in which an evil foreign power shoots down British biplanes with a freighter's secret ray. Believed to have inspired Ronald Reagan's $500 billion laser-beams-in-space ("Star Wars") program because, upon seeing it, he thought it was a documentary.

Q-Planes

Q-Planes II . . . Flying epic that would have followed *Q-Planes* and preceded *Q-Planes III* if it had been made in the 1980s and had starred Sylvester Stallone or Christopher Reeve.

Q.S.Y. . . . Formerly international shorthand code for switching frequencies from one air traffic controller to another. Now merely shorthand code for what pilots feel in strong turbulence.

Quack . . . Sound heard just outside cockpit window on southbound flights in late October.

Quadrant . . . Four rants often uttered by flight instructors in no mood for raves.

Quack

Quash . . . Word used by ABC's Barbara Walters when doing a story about an airline crash.

Quart . . . What pilots of shoestring commuter airlines ask for when refueling truck pulls up.

Quebec . . . Phonetic-alphabet word for letter *Q.* Confusing for Air Canada pilots requesting clearance to land at Ottawa.

Quimby . . . Harriet Quimby, the first American woman to receive a pilot's license, performed an inverted flight over Boston Harbor in 1912, an occasion unfortunately predating the invention of the seat belt.

Quimby

Red Baron . . . Rittmeister Manfred von Richthofen. Though enough of an expert marksman to become Germany's leading ace in World War I, he was such a terrible flyer that he crashed twice during his early training and would have been washed out had it not been for Germany's desperate need for pilots.

Red line . . . Demarcation on tachometer which, if exceeded too often, puts aircraft owner's bank account into the red.

Release . . . A knob or device in cockpit of sailplane that glider pilots activate to free sailplane from towplane while trying to open cockpit vent during takeoff.

Rhumb line . . . Words used by off-duty airline pilots to pick up flight attendants when the pilots are so drunk they cannot even spell "rum."

Rhumb Line

Right Stuff . . . That part of the cockpit equipment on the copilot's side of the aircraft, as in a pilot saying, "You take care of the right stuff. I'll take care of the left stuff."

Roger . . . Name of a pilot.

Roll . . . A pilot whose aileron cables have snapped is said to be on a roll.

Roll out . . . Either recovery from a steep bank, dissipation of speed while landing, or—in some cases—both.

Roger

Runway . . . A mythical place usually fifty aircraft ahead.

Shuttle . . . A cramped, crowded, expensive, retrievable space vehicle that, usually after long delays, rockets off into earth orbit as its passengers attempt to perform tasks and do work under uncomfortable conditions, which sometimes include malfunctioning toilets. Also, the name of a no-frills airline service with similar features.

Sink . . . Atmospheric condition encountered by sailplane pilots that makes them feel as though they're flying one.

Slip . . . Landing technique to compensate for crosswinds in which pilot crosses controls to dramatically reduce lift (see falling rocks).

Slow flight . . . Type of low-altitude flying practiced by student pilots who forget that just because they can fly like birds doesn't mean they can land in trees.

Snaproll . . . What usually happens when you try to roll too quickly.

Soft-field Takeoff . . . Difficult maneuver attempted by jetliner pilots who skid off the runway on rollout.

Slip

Solo . . . That part of a student pilot's training that instructors look forward to the most.

Spin . . . What makes the world go 'round—when you're looking at it directly through windscreen.

Spoiler . . . Means by which sailplanes can decrease lift, usually when instructor hands controls over to student pilot.

Solo

Spruce Goose . . . Name of Howard Hughes's famous World War II jumbo wooden transport. Also, how pilots with the "right stuff" describe low-level flight over pine forests.

Stall . . . A place where student pilots get to spend the night if they continue pulling the stick back despite instructor's yells and screams.

Sucker hole . . . Large hole in cloud cover that disappears as one tries to descend through it. Favorite of VFR pilots, and origin of the phrase, "if God meant for man to fly He wouldn't have created clouds."

Spruce Goose

Tachometer . . . Instrument used by flight attendants sizing up pilots tachy enough to use rhumb lines.

Tail group . . . The airfoil members of the assembly located at the rear of an airplane. Also, businessmen who take seats at the back of a jetliner to watch flight attendants walk up the aisle.

Terminal control area . . . A turnip-shaped section of air space controlled by major metropolitan airports in which general aviation flights are almost always terminated.

Tachometer

That is correct . . . The preferred FAA phrase for reaffirmation, to be uttered over the radio slowly and calmly, as in: "That is correct. I am out of fuel. My landing gear is jammed. And I have an unhappy American bald eagle flying loose in cockpit." Preferred over other phrases such as "reet," "you got it," and "Yankee Echo Alpha Hotel."

Thirty Seconds over Tokyo . . . Holding pattern instruction often given to airline pilots awaiting landing clearance for Los Angeles International Airport.

Thirty Seconds over Tokyo

Towline . . . Persuasive remark used by sailplane pilots who ask motorists to help them drag gliders back to active runways after off-field landings.

Trailing edge . . . What the leading edge of an aircraft becomes after striking other aircraft while taxiing.

Trim tab . . . Soft drink popular with female flyers who wear tight-fitting red jumpsuits.

Trim Tab

Turn-and-bank indicator . . . An amusing device on instrument panel used by flight instructors to helpfully point out to student pilots that it is often unwise to rest heavy feet on rudder pedals.

UFO . . . Unidentified flying object. Flying saucer without a transponder.

Ultimate load . . . The load that will, or is computed to, cause failure in any structural member. For airliners, the Washington Redskins on a return flight after a big post-game dinner.

Turn-and-bank Indicator

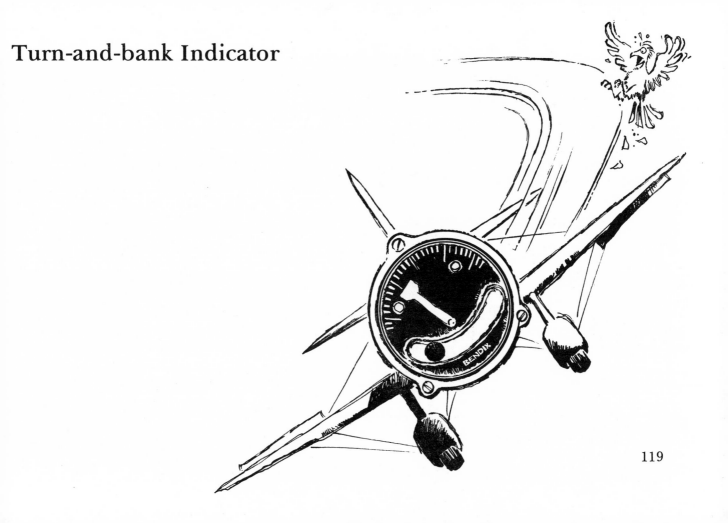

Ultralight . . . A device invented to disprove ancient theory that lawn mowers weren't meant to fly.

Undercarriage . . . Equipment to be found beneath an aircraft making emergency landing near hansom cab lanes in New York's Central Park.

Unicom . . . Radio setting of 122.8 or 123.0 that allows you to chat with seven hundred other pilots as you turn on final in the middle of them.

Ultralight

Unsafe . . . What any flashing red light means, unless, of course, the light is malfunctioning, and everything looks okay, except of course for that big hole in the runway, but that could just be an oil smear, and besides it's getting late and anyway . . .

Up . . . Secret of flight (see Down, secret of crash). Also, chant repeated over and over by pilots trying to clear *USA Today* Building upon take-off from Washington National Airport.

Updraft . . . Polite term for what pilots encounter making low-level flight over smokestacks of U.S. Steel plant in Gary, Indiana (see Inverted flight).

Upddraft

U/S . . . Unserviceable. Peculiar military designation for aircraft that need servicing.

Useful load . . . Any passenger who can take over the controls while the pilot takes a little nap.

Vacuum instruments . . . Instruments that require an internal vacuum to operate. Source of the phrase, "Nature abhors a vacuum."

U/S

Vector . . . Phonetic alphabet for letter *V* as pronounced by air traffic controllers in Texas.

Venturi tube . . . A tube for storing golf clubs.

Vertigo . . . Fear of heights common among pilots who observe wing root snapping off or other phenomena for which space is provided in remarks section of log book. Also, what a pilot with a parachute would say over his radio to an air controller named Ed Vert if his wing root began to go.

Vertigo

VFR (Visual Flight Rules) . . . Those rules followed by novice pilots in taking off and ascending into thick cloud cover.

VHF . . . Very high frequency. Radio channels that permit you to follow audio portion of television soap operas on long cross-country flights.

Viscosity . . . A measurement of the thickness of the oil spewed all over your windscreen.

VOR . . . Very high frequency omnidirectional radio range (see **VHFORR**). Radio gizmo that can give you a course setting away from a place as well as toward it. Very popular with pilots who find themselves over Newark, New Jersey.

Viscosity

V1 . . . Takeoff speed at which a pilot is supposed to be able to stop an aircraft if engine fails and if he hasn't begun takeoff halfway down the runway.

V2 . . . Minimum speed at which aircraft may take off, and probably must because of aircraft landing behind it.

Warning area . . . Portion of international airspace being used by U.S. military for operations, often including all approaches to Bermuda airport. Civilian pilots may proceed through it anyway as international airspace cannot legally be restricted. (Example: civilian pilots were not restricted from flying through the Battle of Midway.)

Warning Area

Wave . . . Strong, continuous, wind-driven updraft in Rocky Mountains. Used by sailplane pilots to ascend to 40,000 feet or higher without an engine, to the delight of passing jetliners. Also, a friendly gesture of farewell made to rich sailplane pilots by their heirs on ground.

Wilco . . . Roger's last name.

Wind correction . . . When wind is from the right, add degrees of correction. When wind is from the left, subtract degrees of correction. When wind is from ahead, subtract from miles travelled. When wind is from above, check out your turn-and-bank indicator.

Wind Correction

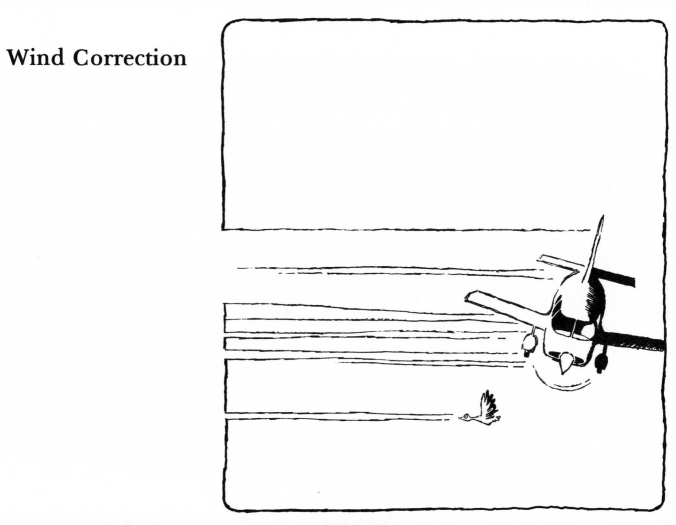

Windsock . . . Wind direction indicator visible to all pilots flying within fifty feet of it if they remember where it's supposed to be. Usually located at opposite end of runway.

Wingchord . . . Strange sound made when wing root is about to go.

Wings of Eagles . . . 1957 flying epic starring John Wayne and Maureen O'Hara. Tells story of Frank "Spig" Wead, famous World War I aviator who later becomes a Hollywood comedy screenwriter. Said to be film responsible for Wayne's return to making westerns.

Wings of Eagles

Wings of Fire . . . 1967 flying epic starring Suzanne Pleshette and James Farentino. Frequently shown on no-frills transatlantic charter flights during electrical storms.

Wings of the Hawk . . . 1953 flying epic starring Van Heflin and Abbe Lane. (Moviegoer quickly discovers it is actually a western about the Mexican revolution.)

Wingstrut . . . Peculiar ritual performed by student pilots upon getting out of low-winged trainers following first flight performed without instructor yelling at them. Usually results in instructor yelling at them.

Wingstrut

X . . . Short for "experimental." Many X-aircraft unfortunately become ex-aircraft.

X-1 . . . Bell aircraft used by Chuck Yeager to become the first pilot to break the sound barrier. The Air Force kept this event a complete secret for years, leading the American public to believe the British broke the sound barrier because of a completely fictitious 1952 flying epic called *Breaking the Sound Barrier.*

X

X-15 . . . 1961 flying epic starring the immortal Richard Donner and Mary Tyler Moore. Set in the early days of a California flight-test base. Would have gotten more than a two-star rating if they had called it *The Right Stuff,* or at least *Breaking the Sound Barrier.*

Xanthus . . . Modern Kinik, principal city of ancient Lycia, situated above the mouth of the Koca River in Antalya il (province), Turkey. Where all lost baggage ends up.

X-15

Xenon . . . Volatile rare gas used in strobe lights. Comes from Greek for "see non," as when light is flashed in front of you.

Xhosa . . . Bantu language spoken by 3,500,000 people in southern Africa—all of them air traffic controllers.

Xocoatl . . . Aztec beverage made from cocoa beans. Origin of ribald saying on Central American airlines: "Coffee, xocoatl, or me?"

Xocoatl

X-ray . . . Phonetic alphabet word used by skydivers discussing what they're going to do after the jump.

X-wing fighter . . . Imaginary space combat vehicle used in fantasy movie *Star Wars,* which when viewed by Ronald Reagan prompted him to order it into production.

Xyelidae . . . Family of sawflies of the order *Hymenoptera,* class Insecta. Has nothing to do with airplanes, but fills up *X* quota in this book.

X-ray

MEDICAL
COVERAGE

Yak . . . Russian propellor-driven fighter named and designed after large ox. Quickly phased out early in Korean War. Also, contents of most cockpit in-flight recorders.

Yang . . . On Chinese aircraft, right rudder pedal.

Yak

Yankee . . . Phonetic alphabet word used by customs officials at Latin American airports and air traffic controllers in South Carolina.

Yaw . . . Another phrase used by air traffic controllers in South Carolina. As in, "Yaw stand by, hear?"

Yaw string . . . Piece of yarn affixed to the windscreen of sailplanes to assist in turn coordination. Some student pilots have made entire flights without the yaw string budging from its proper position, usually by sneakily affixing both ends of the yarn to the windscreen with glue.

Yankee

Yeager . . . Commonly regarded as the greatest flier in history, test pilot Chuck Yeager was the first man to break the sound barrier, but he was unknown to the general public until he appeared as a bartender in the movie *The Right Stuff;* fried eggs on a hot engine cowling for a television commercial; and inspired the leather flight-jacket fad that was quickly all the rage in the most chi-chi districts of Manhattan.

Yellow dog . . . What Charlie Blue Leader and Red Fox One fighter pilots call a wingman who turns back to base because he forgot his Dramamine tablets.

Yeager

YI . . . International aircraft marking for Iraqi aircraft. Also, what Iranian pilots say upon seeing one.

Yin . . . On Chinese aircraft, left rudder pedal.

Yoke . . . What makes Scandinavian Air Lines pilots laugh.

Zzzzzzzzzz . . . Often the last sound heard on playback of tapes from wrecked aircrafts' cockpit flight recorders.

Zzzzzzzzzz

Zephyr . . . A type of gentle breeze last recorded at Chicago's O'Hare International Airport for five minutes on May 21, 1960. Also the name of a train popular with airline passengers on days when O'Hare breezes are not so gentle.

Zeppelin . . . Famous type of German lighter-than-airship. Proved at Lakehurst, New Jersey, that balloons are just as dangerous even with engines.

Zero-zero . . . Short for zero ceiling, zero visibility. An atmospheric condition named after the fuel tank reading often seen at the same time.

Zeppelin

Zig-zag . . . Strange flight pattern on final approach favored by student pilots attempting a crab or slip for the first time.

Zilch . . . Short term for either altitude or fuel supply.

Zoom . . . Sound a low-flying aircraft makes when coming out of dive into a high-angle climb before striking trees and making a different sound.

Zig-zag

Zulu . . . African word for the exact time in Greenwich, England.

Zumwalt . . . Former chief of naval operations famous for letting Navy carrier crews grow beards and moustaches until they discovered how itchy facial hair can be under oxygen masks.

The End